Eternity or Equivalent

Also by James Milenkovic and published by Ginninderra Press
Salt & Petals

James Milenkovic

Eternity or Equivalent

Eternity or Equivalent
ISBN 978 1 76041 557 0
Copyright © text James Milenkovic 2018
Cover photo: old room © vlntn

First published 2018 by
GINNINDERRA PRESS
PO Box 3461 Port Adelaide 5015
www.ginninderrapress.com.au

Contents

Darkness and Light	9
Happiness	11
When We Touch	12
Lovers in the Park	13
Attractants	14
Haunt	15
Eclipse	17
Your Voice	18
Ballerina	19
10 April 2010	21
Lights	23
Sometimes	24
Erasure	25
Wishes	26
Laugh	27
Hot Air Balloon	28
How I Love You	30
How It Is	31
First Christmas	33
Away	34
Desire	35
Fathers and Sons	36
After It	37
Horses	38
Lonely Corridors	39
Where I Go	41
Attic	42
He and I	43
What Is the Past?	44

Cemetery	45
Fracture	46
Summer Boy	47
Almost	48
Studio	49
Watching	50
Transparent	52
The Swing in the Garden	53
Lost Child	54
Take Care	55
Pickings	56
Guillermo	57
Dying Fire	58
Dust and Dirt	**59**
Vegetable Garden	61
Homebody	62
Thirst	64
A Conversation	65
The Towel	67
Moth	69
When He Takes My Arm	70
Under	71
Gallery Lady	72
Attrice	73
Autumnal Road	74
Carpet	75
Amber	76
Dialogue	77
The Dress	78
Switch	79
Housework	80

Express	81
Earth and Sky Kiss	82

Through Our Hands   83

Sunday Roasts	85
Collecting	86
Sprinkled Field	87
Ode to Onyx	88
Mindfulness	89
Stitches	91
Love Fool	92
Rain on Tin	93
Forest	94
Bubble About to Burst	95
Sitting in a Waiting Room	96
Path	98
Out	99
Siblings	100
Cyclone	101

Illusory Highway   103

Shedding	105
Question	106
Piano	107
On My Skin	108
Pearl	109
Mind's Making	110
Stay	111
Onwards	112
Letter	113
The Beginning of Desire	114
M	115
On My Father	116

Lesson	117
Ministering	118
Kiss	119
Innocence	120
Longing	121
Ladybird	122
Habitual	123
Dollhouse	124
Cornell's Boxes	125
Next To Him	126
Incoming	127
Her Grandmother's Necklace	128
Fast Boy	129
Dramaturgic	130
Gran's Chair	131
Your Face	132
Tea	133
Moonlit Room	134
Flower	135
Moh	136
Later	137

Darkness and Light

Happiness

Gladness
    is not seen in any arena of life
as that of a dog
going for his leisurely walk.
That exultant look in his eyes as he marches,
hops
    and skips
across the grass,
    bold and handsome,
propeller tail slicing the air like a blade,
mouth ajar in a jubilant beam   and salmon tongue
tasting the seasoning of the surrounds.

The eager movement made by his
four-limbed body,
    that swagger
despite materiality
or tokens.

His happiness comes from the most modest of things:
sun, air, sky
and perhaps a bone.

The ease,
the lack of triviality he knows –
    it is much to be desired.

When We Touch

When our fingers prickle from one another's magnetism –
teased   and enticed
by an invisible voltage –
and our hands interlock as though indissoluble,
    the orbit of countless galaxies are broken.

When we touch our bodies burn,
coursing like a fervent blaze
in a swirling union of oxygen and flame
   through desiccated countryside.

In taking your hand I revel:
meeting   despite the black hole expanse,
   finding   beyond hope
      adoring   what I'm privileged
to touch.

Lovers in the Park

Two young men on the park bench
sharing a look I know well –

though proximate, thirsting to flit
and fuse
in one another's expanse;

fingers stealing brushes in moments
it feels safe to do so;
laughter
enabling them to curl
into each other –

that rush of excitement.

Even without knowing them,
I can see it in these two men –

the resonant presence of being
utterly intoxicated off one another.

Attractants

With his cerulean mantle and fan of spotted plumage,
the peacock is a grandstanding creature –
self-assured in his impressiveness,
    plucky with ostentation.

Bold,
owing to his handsomeness,
the peafowl hasn't reluctance in seeking,
        or difficulty in securing,
a mate –
rendezvous are all this ornamented
bird offers.

No long
or lifetime offer like Adélie penguins:
    arbitrary aestheticism is the peacock's game –
using   quite expertly
the interplay of iridescence,
angle
    and light
to conquer any aspirant mate
that comes before him.

Haunt

Though you've gone,
reminiscences of you linger,
small phantoms that haunt me,
    have become stained in the ecology of this dwelling
and are inescapable.

Inhaling the ghost molecules
of the air you breathed;
your aftershave clings to the fibres of
pillow and doona in the bedroom.
Sometimes
I lie and gulp the fragrant notes in,
feeling
the syrupy sweetness swirl through my nostrils,
      down the tunnel of my throat.

Like soldiers, your books stand guard on the shelf,
washed in soft morning sun;
a shirt –
    crinkled –
shoulders the occasional chair,
and in the chambers of the bathroom cupboard,
your toiletries, potions
    and brews await their errand in the morning routine.

Sometimes,
I am certain that I hear the heavy patters
of your bare feet on the floorboards,
    or see your shadow cast itself on the ivory walls.
But this is just scotoma,
the trick of eye and mind.
This home,
has become a house without you.
An authored space that has had its chief character
plucked
out of the plot   when our story had only just begun.

Eclipse

We turn our faces towards from the sky,
the orb of shimmering rock
succumbing to a malignant veil
of black.

Unfathomable to imagine,
       to see,
darkness conquering light.

Your Voice

Far more than air expulsing through pharynx
and larynx,
your voice is
    the crisp coolness of ocean air
        carried cross tides of jade, sapphire and teal.
It rises above the monotony
to incise like razors
and later soothe with its velvety warmth.
Your voice is
    the passing of words through pillars of porcelain,
        into the atmosphere of humanity
a whispery song
that haunts
    and enraptures
        when it reaches   my ear,
the nearest to heaven
I will ever be.

Ballerina

She is a fantastical creature
this woman (or swan) I watch from the
darkness,
       her poise   exquisite,
thin and
long.

Her aura is both alluring and terrifying,
    physical but ethereal;
she burns through the space,
twirling and
       soaring
in a blaze of feather, skin and tulle.

The score climaxes.

    Her delicacy of movement interweaves
with the jarring violence
of cleaving hands,
crisp lines,
the gruelling hours of training,
and rigidity of nourishment,
       all unrecognised (or forgotten)
in this moment.

Then her rhythm,
    her blaze within the milieu   decelerates
and,
    en pointe,
she comes to centre stage.
    The movement
concludes.

The score
ends
in crackling applause roars.

10 April 2010

When I didn't see him
I dreamt about him, and
when I saw him,
I'd dream about him anyway.
He,
for so long,
was my ghost.

That night my dream was made real
sitting alongside him –
    the holiest of places for me.
Robbed of sagacity,
the dark romanticised his glow,
his smell,
his body –
a work of art appreciated only in the dark.
Potholes in the road,
granted me seconds of
       heaven.

And you should know,
Even if she's the one behind your cage of ribs,
if her song is the one you hum in the warmth of your throat.
    Just let me be the thought,
floating

indelible on the ocean of your mind.

If I could do it again,
I would dare to take his hand –
the boy's whose touch was fire and voice,
              honeyed –
and whisper,
I love you.
Because burning with desire in silence
is the greatest punishment I can endure.

Lights

The highest point of the crest

offers a outlook on the smoky

black swath

        detail   depth   distance

drenched in opacity.

The city lights twinkling, pixellated,

with a kaleidoscopic delight that punctures

the dimness –

offering a life   beyond me

looking out

        and wanting in.

Sometimes

i suppose
that most times i am happy,
my days spent occupied
with monotonous happiness

then night comes
and day loses its flavour
and i am reminded of absences.
lying in bed, sunken in sadness,
i do think about the things i miss

and never having
the mettles to do or say what it takes
i'll pen a poem,
so should you read it,
you will know.

Erasure

The needle didn't hurt as much as this light.
Numbed with feeling,
I mustn't have registered its bore
and buzz.

With each laser pulse, permanence shatters,
foreign pathogens explode,
    free radicals in my blood –
the surface suggestion of your name becomes
evanescent.

While your exterior mark will peter out
    and carnal pain remains residual,
what of your internal stain?
No beam,
no blade
can burrow deep enough;

only time will tell.

Wishes

It's your birthday.
The party,
    procession and kerfuffle,
the obligatory cake and gifts from family
and friends (if fortunate enough to have any).

Please
I don't want this hoopla,
the exhaustion of energy,
    money changing hands for material drivel
and me feigning excitement
when what I truly desire
cannot be purchased
or bargained.

Why celebrate another year
of not adding up to very much?

Laugh

To hear your laugh,
> its burbling, jovial rhythm,

I would traverse through all that is dark and nightmarish
on earth.

Beyond my corporeal architecture –
> below cavernous cellular growth –

your laugh unlocks gates to my spirit,
bringing light to the darkest shades of blue
> and black. Its infectious tone and timbre sparks a wild fire

that sets the kindling of my heart ablaze,
> fuelling my body's machine.

And so I must be with you –
> affix myself to your glow as a moth does a bulb,

like a parasite does its host –
to live,
> to breathe

to be saved.

Hot Air Balloon

A belch of scorching flame
into the gaseous dome
and we ascend
    like prayers
into the crispness of the morning.

Up
    and up,
greeting the tang of purple,
yellow and grey clouds,
        feeling the warm kiss of sunshine
on our skin,
the air heavy with ice frosting our
bronchi with each inhale.

I am trepid to begin with,
my legs shuddering,
loathe to peer out
from the basket that contains us –
       to be so   far
      removed from the staunchness of the earth
        free from its comforting confines;

    The world below is a dreamy haze from which,
miraculously,
we have been lifted;
this vantage from eye of bird,
    or God,
offers a heartening release
(however short)
from complication and
the discordance of life

Up
    and up,
        further
we soar.

How I Love You

The foundations of my love aren't ephemeral like skin,
mathematical alike the geometry of skyscrapers,
or ineffectual like the crush of some imprudent teen.
My love for you is a force unchallengeable by anything on earth
or heaven.

I love you with intent and ardour.
Tolerant on your drug, only you can gratify
this insatiable need,
only you can placate the demand symptomatic of withdrawal.

I love you with hope and agenda, however selfish it may be.
My planetary body necessitates the symmetry of your orbit,
the rational arrangement of my pieces with yours.

I love you blindly and unquestionably.
There is no doubting the workings that have united us,
without you, I exist only in body
and my soul   forever tethered to yours,
will wander
        until the end of time.

How It Is

Here is the languid mother,
    shepherding her young children amid the herd
of Saturday shoppers,
and pushing the cumbersome trolley
        with its busted wheel
            along.

It's an exercise in anxiety,
subduing curious hands,
    steering them back to the safety of the trolley,
fearing the shock,
the gushing calamity of them smashing a jar of pasta sauce.

The journey was charged
with the cacophony of screaming   laughing
crying,
the notion of quiet,
      however brief,
totally inconceivable to these beasts –
    God, how she wishes for it.

Her forehead shines with perspiration,
hair slips from its tight ponytail,
    her daughter in purple tugs eagerly for recognition.
She's quick to chastise,
    more vehement than she would be at home.

And now somebody,
    maybe everybody,
is looking,
critiquing her maternal shortcomings.

She leaves.
There's enough food at home for dinner tonight.

First Christmas

From the bowed cardboard box
       dormant these eleven months
we finally come to take out
the seasonal decorations   in a ruffle,
   jingle
and swirl
of glitter and kitschiness.

The shapely pine mounted in the corner –
fragrant and lush –
   awaits dressing:
      a centrepiece were parcels
wrapped in sleek and
patterned paper,
      pressed and creased   with adoring hands,
will find lodging.

Over wine
and takeaway pizza we adorn this hero:
   tinselled
and ornamented –
   an act that is the marrow in our love's bones;
the building blocks of a memory,
installed in fondness,
   to be cupped tenderly in our hands –

our first Christmas.

Away

The paint around the door frame
falls like flakes,
    assembling in piles
at the skirting

fine cracks in the porcelain
plaster, wrinkled,
        crated and crumbled. The room holds
the uneasy mood,
knickknacks tinkle and   tremble

the kettle boiling,
    the dog, unknowing, wags his tail
after

you slam the door.

Desire

I want more than my hands can amass
in their fervent seizing,
    though not of possessions.
    I want the infinity of sky,
    lack of inhibition and sovereignty.

I want life and all its avenues,
    to explore the golden pastures of success
and triumph
but also to amble down darkened alleyways
of disillusionment and ill-doings,
feel
the sticky discomfort of erring.

I want my life to be more
than is now.

These years consigned to me I want gratified,
      to not wake
after years' long torpor
and see   that I have neglected
to live.

Fathers and Sons

A boy –
    no older than six –
clings to his father in the food court at Highpoint,
        wrapping his arms around him,
almost pestering in his imploration
for notice.
    It makes me wonder

what have I missed out on?

The amorous display continues,
this little boy besotted by his dad's presence:
infantile fingers contour the skin
lined with age and experience,
    markers of a life lived   a narrative I won't ever know.

Both of us knowing
this is the fathers we will be –
doting
    as ours never were,
recompensing
    for the love we weren't ever given,
accepting
    the way ours could never be.

After It

I am first to wake
and greet the sun
      whitewashing your bedroom.

On the floor,
the threads and peelings of last night's clothes,
    stained
with decaying sweat
        and cologne.
Your limbs of fingers
searching   for my lips
    to then fall   fluid across the cambers
and nooks of my body. Swimming   in the waters of each other
until eternity became an hour.

Now,
arches of light dance across your face –
slumbering body calm
    and mind –
reconnoitring one last dream
before you wake
      to kiss me or kill me.

Horses

Emerging from the urban highway,
        declining the crest's steepness,
I come into a span of ghost gums and ironbarks,
with chimneyed homes yoked amongst them.
I pull the car over
across from two horses,
idling
      unjacketed in their paddock
          strange and enchanting beasts;

I call one and obligingly,
it approaches,
tottering through the grass, evaluating me
gauging the vibration of my aura,
   is he trustworthy?

His long head reaches over the wire fence,
I offer my hand,
tentatively stroking the long muzzle,
   unlike the texture of my dog
      (the only animal with which I can draw comparison),
the horse's coat resembles under-brushed velvet.

Why have I,
   uneducated in equinity,
found myself here?
Perhaps its because I recognise in both our souls
   the desire to live.

Lonely Corridors

Where I Go

The café is busy today (as it is every day at this time, I presume).
An arbitrariness to this moment,
patrons coming together
at this particular place,
        at this particular time,
        a nonrecurring pattern
of here now
and gone tomorrow.

I'm fulfilled by the warmth I find here,
the clinking of cups on saucers,
    the hiss of the machine   busy with production,
the unremitting current of conversation.
But for me,
the café's appeal lies in its capacity
to render my loneliness mute.

Perhaps that's why I come here.
Yes,
it's definitely why I do
      (even with the praiseworthy coffee),
to lithely slip myself into someone else's story,
ponder,
over the creamy aeration of milk and chocolate dusting,
the triviality of it all,
    become the character in a narrative I overhear somebody tell,
        enticed by the prospect of being as far from myself
            as possible.

Attic

The attic is a chamber of unused artefacts,
or worse,
forgotten ones.
A dank roof space
rousing an inherent uneasiness,
       reviving a panorama   of items shrouded
with threads of cobwebs and sheets of dust,
   quiet,
cluttered.

High above
the warmth and furnishings where the living
pass every moment
through corridors and rooms –
   sounds familiar and organic –
like platelets through the vein of home.

Minimal in its trimmings,
the room is angular in line and shape,
   its high-ceilinged dullness
uninviting,
   neglected.

You linger in the corner.

He and I

Traces of sunset pucker the long,
    low horizon,
exposing its wildfire scars
on the choppy surface of the ocean

but it is dusk's consuming blueness –
        deep and dark –
that anonymises us as we walk
barefoot
on the shoreline.

The voluble rumble of waves
conjoin with the overhead cries
of water birds;
        sharp and salty wind frenzies   crash
into our skin,
    exposed like limestone outcrops
from beneath our warm-wear.

Your face
in this chiaroscuro light,
    the open arms of the ocean,
the newness of this adventure –

I am lost with you tonight.

What Is the Past?

Is it forgotten,
buried deep in
cold black dirt,
slipped from memory's ledge   offside
in the field of consciousness?

The past is the future
not yet repeated. We can't evade the
searchlights of previous things by
hiding
    in the dark,
safe and comfortable in our forgetting.

Our challenge –
perhaps our greatest – is stepping   out
    from the pernicious lure of disremembering,
accepting onus
and finding
a new plateau on which to ground
our lives.

Cemetery

I sometimes walk through the cemetery,
on the hallowed ground where those who've gone before
lie beneath cenotaphs of engraved marble and granite,
memorialised through bouquets
and photographs
    carefully
        thoughtfully placed
by their doting commemorators.

I don't view this place, as others often do,
with morbidity or dismay,
instead
    I come here to wander
           (ghost-like myself)
for the silence unique
to this locale,
    where life meets death,
not as enemies, but equals.

The cemetery grants me peace;
a sanctuary from the tumult of
living,
where I am never alone and never in company.
Just myself in this equidistant dimension.
From here, I might take revelations   back
to the ordered clutter
of my study   overlooking the apple orchard –
    abundant with red and glossy riches – and
bring to life the stories that,
without my scribing,
are otherwise   lifeless.

Fracture

Mind elsewhere,
it slips between my fingers
in an eternal plunge to definite disaster –

that sound.

Commotion and confusion
consequent,
time splits in the splintering.

One hundred thousand fractals   disperse across
the floor.
Some specks of glitter
so small that neither fingertips nor brush can offer
    salvation,
cannot placate this mistake,
or make right that which was broken.

Summer Boy

I met him again in summer school.
He sat with me in the park
and at the beach –
    glances triggered
skipping heartbeats
        and exchanges at lunch

in shorts and tee
he was relaxed and blithe,
        belonging to another boy.

    Though my lips never met his,
we never rebuffed
each others' lumbering search
    for contact.

Almost

This bed,
waffled with doona and blanket
    where we have lain every night –
exploring the pastures
        and intricacies
of one another's bodies –
has become the meeting point of
forms too fearful,
too proud
    to touch.

Like dusk and night,
we share   only a moment
    (those passing hours
before the darkness deepens) –
    never perpetual
        yet so frustratingly
close
like
fingers of new lovers, daring to knot
in the safe and
    forgiving case of dark.

Studio

The artist's studio, refurbished from
its former life as the concrete and red brick shed,
    is settled beneath the backyard overgrowth of wisteria and maple
where roughly at noon,
the sun spills through the mottled windows
and bathes the space in a pool of lemony incandescence.

The studio is provisioned with all the requisite materials:
brushes, easel, palette and paper,
    (bearing that delectable arty smell).
It is the noisiest and quietest place on earth,
where visions and subjects
demand
        I heed their calls

An almost spiritual ether where one might, in solitude,
wait out
the hubbub of the world, or
pause
for the clarity of thoughts to flow
like a clear stream
of paint.

Watching

Have you ever taken a moment to watch people
passing by,
to truly see them, their rapport between self and other?
Those fleeting encounters –
       near-immediate shifts in seasons –
intrigue and
       pull me into the way we navigate
the days we are assigned.

What can be gauged by their passing? Mostly a superficial
understanding,
       a surface judgement –
but if one looks assiduously enough,
one can see   small things,
details
that could shape a narrative of the subject   or possibly allude
to a richer, more comprehensive understanding
of their reality.

A backpack is slung to one side, weight burdened
to the left rather than distributed equally;
       the small tear in what seems like an expensive jacket –
a gift perchance?
Its wearer is too busy or slothful
to mend it with needle and thread,
yet not wanting it thrown out
    with the oddments of life.

Watching is understanding,
viewing
the intricacies and circulatory entanglements we share,
    a tethering to flesh and earth,
though varied.

Watching
is questioning,
asking why things are as they are.
Watching
is an art,
a gentle practice of finding
        and appreciating beauty
in the everyday.

Transparent

What has happened
in my life

that causes me
to artlessly love

anyone

who shows me
the smallest trace

of kindness?

Do I know so little
of affection,

have I experienced so few
instances of it,

that I am imprudent enough
to make real

a visitation of hopeless love?

The Swing in the Garden

Enter through the ligneous door,
        disguised by twisting ivy,
then cross the wild garden and sit atop the swing
hanging
from the crusty limb of the ash.

A missile, you split the air –
    clean and crisp –
descending like a pendulum's swing;
with each rise
and fall
the wind ripples
        and washes
across your body like a swell,
murmuring its song into the conical foldings
of your ears.

Let the swinging palliate
your symptoms.

    Soar   with all the ease you can muster,
higher and higher
        to forget,
just for now,
        what you know.

Lost Child

Gone
quickly as a splice of light,
itinerant steps
    logical brain quelled
by panic's erratic beating,
voice calling out,
    in decibels unknown.

Child gone. Child taken.
Body heavy,
down,
no longer ambulatory.
Where is
she?

Take Care

Your words,
       whether shaped like glass
or petals,
stake a settlement in my heart
and are unmovable

forever circulating around
its circulatory halls,
   replaying
like a film on rerun.

One shape of breath
through the teeth by the tongue
has the capacity to ruin
or save

so please,
take care with what you say,
       because I haven't it in me
to love again.

Pickings

I am in a cavalcade of suitors,
men who are blood sporting
for their next love
(more like conquest).

While they may catch my eye,
charm with their loquaciousness over free-flowing drinks,
there'll be no affair between us,
because while latent lovers are everywhere

no one will do
but you.

Guillermo

I have not been to the circus since I was six,
remembering so vividly the performing bear
that brought such harrowing to my heart:
his emaciated form stammering through the arena door,
fur patched and threadbare,
      like a carpet that's born too much traffic.

He was to perform and
delight the crowd,
beneath a seizure of flashing lights, raucous music,
      painted and dressed like a weeping clown,
   (completely neglecting his anguish his immense sadness that I,
an unknowing child,
could in somehow intuit).

I am dismayed to think that I –
by being in attendance –
was complicit to such abject humiliation of this previously regal creature;
I am loath to think of him,
Guillermo,
      prodded back to his iron settlement,
surely chained and muzzled,
deprived of sustenance and the entitlement of ease.

A criminal has a better life than him.

Dying Fire

Party's over
    nearing midnight and the
fire has had its stint.

Kindling runs with veins of shining gold,
barely breathing flame,
    the flute thick with plaque of soot and smoke

        Splash of water
hiss and squeal
    and steam
then dark.

Dust and Dirt

Vegetable Garden

The treasures in the soil are ready
to be retrieved.
The labour of planting, watering
    and tending to sprouts and scions,
as well as fending off irksome creepy-crawlies and slugs
with pellet and potion,
will now be satisfied.

Oriented on their stakes,
the greenery of tomato vines
sends perfume rising up
    (strongest amongst the crops)
jewelled with blood red and shiny flesh.

Pull the hair on a carrot's head to see a wink
of orange beneath the loam of mycelium;
    pumpkins hiding behind their leaves,
umbilical on vines   while
potatoes are nuggeted in the dirt,
requiring blind digging
        and a little brush off.

Our vegetable garden
so prosperous with its offerings,
means meals prepared in earnest now,
    cooked with deference for the seasonal abundance,
eaten and enjoyed by those who enter
this house.

Homebody

The arrival of winter
never fails to make me slip into the nesting comforts of home.
I enter into a kind of hibernation,
hoping to elude the encircling days
of grey and cold
and endless rain.

    It's an inane game of hide and seek in which I
am never the victor.

I am filled with a warming pride to think
of this ancient house protecting its inhabitants,
its weatherboard body standing against the onslaught
of season. And though arthritic foundations groan,

    its skin of ceiling permeable to patchy seepages,
it embraces us dependably
like mother's loving arms.

The warmth of the hearth becomes a gathering place
for the home's natives and those who visit:

    conversations are had over freshly brewed tea, or,
armed with a good book,
burrowing the sofa, to be joined by the pup,
who lolls on the woven rug below,

    paws neatly folded inwards so the fire warms his belly.

Days are long here
>   especially in winter.

The pale light of morning falls fluidly across the kitchen,
shifting throughout the day to submerge other spaces and corners
>   in pools of light and shadow.

Sometimes I forgo television and music and simply watch
nature's theatrics from the bay windows.

I watch
>   how the rain gathers into craters of relief-sculpted earth
>   to form

patchy ponds of cloudy passion,

observe
>   the sharp maelstroms of wind savage the forest of pines

so they genuflect like the most devout worshippers.

The arrival of winter
never fails to make me slip into the nesting comforts of home.

Thirst

lips
cracked canyons

an arid mouth that speaks
    of thirst for

you,
a molecule of rescue –

splash,

flowing cool
      on this parched crevice:

I drink you.

A Conversation

I cannot say
as others sometimes do, that your existence
is evidenced by beauty,
      the splendour of the world,
because rationally,
incontestably,
it must also be apparent in the vulgar,
the terrible,
    the deathly.

Pray understand,
it would be reassuring to know
you are there –
not just an elusive figure in the ethos of scepticism –
    and that all those pleas
and covenants
aren't just filling the space,
            the solemn hours
of some naïve fool.

Even so
I'm nonplussed to think that
              when I die,
I will not know heaven,
because I conduct my life in a way that
abhors you;

              but
gracious and forgiving,
surely you   wouldn't permit the
hate that festers,
    that gnaws and guides the most pious of your flock
to hate me   and others
like me?

Surely
    you wouldn't do that.

The Towel

In my villa bathroom
I pull a towel from its burnished perch after showering,
draping myself not only in its crisp rectangle
    of starchiness,
but the narrative of how it has come
to impress my skin.

I feel the richness of its tale –
the hours of sun warming and bleaching the fibres of cloth,
suspended on the line,
      tousling about in the dry wind,
consumed with longing for spring's bouquet,
but caught
in summer's arid grasp.

Has it felt the bore sprinklers' sprays
'round the buffalo patch?
Reprieved only by the interjections of children
frolicking in the squirts –
that trickling, teasing arc of rainbow.

The chorus of birds' songs are written on the staff
of the pile. I hear their melodious chirps and tweets;
    songs of victory about a new current on which to
rise
and soar.

I wonder about the one who laundered the article,
transporting it to and from its tightrope adventures,
to be pressed
and folded
by hands   probably uncaring about the poetry of their task
but appreciated by me nonetheless.

I who stand
wrapped in its cotton brine
    wonder
and give thanks.

Moth

Little moth on my windowpane,
tiny insect intruder,

you are not like your companions
who dive and lunge

at any patch of light –
you are curious.

I offer you my fingertip
so that you may board it

and fly away, but you are intent
on resisting me,

scuttling further down the glass
with powdery flutterings.

Don't you know my intentions are benign?
Why do you elect to stay within these walls

when you are offered the bounty
of the outside world?

Your threads of legs affix to me
and gently I carry you to the back door

where the new wash of wind incites
your mottled wings
and you fly away.

When He Takes My Arm

In public he takes my arm,
ignorant of wondering or condemnatory eyes.

I'm moved by this gesture,
that such an action doesn't warrant calculation
    or inference –
it is as organic as breathing,
simple,
perfunctory.

When he takes my arm
the austerity of the act belies my reaction
to it. It is a declaration
that we are paired,
that the love of two men,
    deserves to be seen.

Under

We reach the wreck,
    barnacled and besieged by a rusty crust,
its hull submerged beneath mounts of white sand,
looking like a magnified version of the domestic decoration
seen in a fishbowl.

As we snorkel,
we become spectators and performers in the marine theatre,
navigating discordant highways of fish,
    who seem surprisingly unruffled by us,
sculptures of coral in auroras of colour,
the weltering jungle of sea grass.

Looking up
to the spectacular play of light
that quavers   and cleaves on the rippling
surface of sapphire,
    I found that to my incredulity,
everything liquesces
in the boroughs of the sea.

Up we rise
to that streak of white, passing
through that interstitial film and
break
    into the urgency of day.

Gallery Lady

The lady at the art gallery is dour in demeanour,
clad in a masculine uniform
of Prussian blue with red trimming.

Her eyes dart between patrons as she patrols the space,
assuring that order is kept,
that everyone maintains the ethos of silent appreciation,
    the sanctified atmosphere, undisturbed.

Of course the gallery holds that air
of pomposity,
where the cultured and chic assemble.
        She abhors children and young people entering this white cube,
steering sticky fingers back,
    demanding the deletion of unpermitted photographs

She's passed these paintings by
a hundred times –
    her mind unchallenged.
What appreciation is there left any more?

Attrice

In photos she smiles,
and at gatherings, enthrals,

    arresting and delighting those around her
with her animated bravado,
    slipping
        and falling
in a stupor of silliness.

She would have it this way –
    she must –
because to not smile, not to laugh and
act
unflappably happy
might let others see
    beyond the curtain of her facade,
realise there is nothing
           spectacularly affable or infectious
about her.

She is plain, and broken, drudging through
the monotony of her life,
           dissatisfied but trying,
cleaving to the hope that
      her fabricated cheerfulness she exerts will
one day
    become unstintingly true.
Even if no one else does, she believes it.
She has to.

Autumnal Road

A curling rim of road
    ablaze with   yellow and
        orange and
              red

        some call them angry colours
      but I think not.

They dance
    and frolic
into the fiery loch below,
arrestingly beautiful,
      without complication
    or question

      joyous and lovely
          riding the wind, tentative as a newborn
      learning to walk.

Carpet

At 15 Dobell Avenue,
the '70s shag of ochre and cream is
thin
as the underbelly of a mongrel,

its ribbed crispness now unpicked,
trodden and pasty
by the couch
like the remnants of roadkill

stains disclose an eating place,
meals and booze consumed
in front of the 6 p.m. news,

evidence of an eremite
living a lonely life,
passing into nothingness because
no one,
    not even I,
mourns his absence.

Amber

A mosquito,
      skilful and aerodynamic hunter,
comes to a cool landing on a parched branch,
abdomen full
with the scarlet succulence of its unsuspecting host.

Above,
   a globule of gelatinous resin prepares
to plunge
under the weight of its own stickiness;
it is then, as fate would have it,
that the mosquito itself,
is engulfed
      by the golden blood
    of the tree.

A millennium later,
the balm has hardened   to stone,
the insect entombed,
   perfectly intact,
petrified in its last, unsuspecting moment
         within
     Earth's own time capsule.

Dialogue

From the day we acquire the ability to think
and articulate our thoughts to the world
and those around us,
we become enmeshed in a lifelong dialogue with
ourselves.

The longest conversation we will ever have,
speaking with this other at every moment,
until our last breath departs and the world
        slips away.

There is no evading
the one who reminds us of what needs doing next,
that confidant to whom we reveal our deepest anxieties,
    elusive and intimate minutiae,
safe only in the fortification of our minds,
vexing us with the immutability of reality.

Still,
it is comforting to know I am on no occasion
    alone,
(strictly speaking).

I take solace in the recognition that
although my inelegant and incoherent mouth may not form
words   feelings   emotions   as I might wish,
    they are ample, well-formulated
and heard
in the mechanism of my mind.

The Dress

Procuring the dress was an event,
an exercise in anxiety and tedium
(how any woman enjoys
    frivolously perusing boutiques stupefies her),
the sole consolation was that she had months
to prepare.
It seemed far too expensive for this single wearing;
in hindsight,
one could have been borrowed from a friend and
searching could've been eliminated. Her mind was
occupied with other things.

Draping from its modest hanger
a stream of black fabric lies limp on the quilt.
    She stares at it,
a blemish on the room's complexion
of creams, bones, and beiges,
so horrendously   stark and
    incompatible
against the sunlight irradiating the room
on this magnificent day.

Just looking at it causes a visual assault,
a knotting in the throat.

Still
the dress will do nicely.
    It will serve its purpose well,
help her play her bereaved part
convincingly.

Switch

I am troubled to think
of someone –
      a stranger –
staying in my home while I am not there,
saturating it with their own moods and narration,
    foreign to its intimacies and the ghosts
    I am so conversant with.

I stop at the verge of this new home's door,
timid to enter   and proclaim it as my
domain.
Though its aura is different from my own home
I detect the same constituents:
the warmth of love in this place permeates,
while the marks and scuffs of living
wreathe walls and floor,
making it
more homely, more enticing,
and revealing the care and pride that resides here.

We share an understanding –
      my counterpart and I –
an awareness of residency
(however brief)
in one another's dwelling.

Housework

I enjoy cleaning my home,
the satisfaction of seeing sense
and order
restored to sullied
    and wayward items.

The knowledge that love and love has been taken,
energy spent
in the rendering of tidiness.

Keeping house allows me to reconnect
with its verse –
    natural rhythms and tones –
our intimate dialogue,
so extraordinarily personal.

I feel immense pride upon finishing,
contentedness and clarity of mind,
    knowing
that if I can make order
here
then surely   I can smooth away
other
more asinine troubles.

Express

I caught the last train from the station,
    divested of treasures and belongings,
the most impetuous thing I've done –
no anticipation of how long I'd stay
              or if I'd return.
The thought of being rootless and ungrounded
didn't disquiet me.
I've been forlorn all my life.

The train pitched and trundled on its tracks,
moving through the cool dark like a worm
             burrowing in the moistness
of dirt,
nothing discernible in the abstractedness of speed,
      except the blot of occasional station lights
as the chariot of liberty
rolls on, and soon

the hiss of brakes,
the stink of diesel,
and I'm here
    in the heart of this city, which beats
with zealous intensity,
under the screaming kaleidoscope of colour
    and possibility.
I am so lost.

Earth and Sky Kiss

nocturnal hummock
sitting submerged like a shipwreck
in the inky lesions of blue, grey and green.

horizon blurs
under this triumvirate of colour –
ground and sky come together,
kiss
in synchronisation,
as settlements up ahead become dusty
              and unsharpened
in the surrealist shroud.

driving along the illusory highway,
    mechanical beams slice through the dim,
parting the feathery markings,
so soft,
they're surely made by angels' wings.

Through Our Hands

Sunday Roasts

With each slice of beef
I am taken back

to my childhood. My family assembled
at the table for this quotidian ritual

(father at the head,
drunk again), for another meal

to be taken in bristling silence before
censure   raised voices,

the old man retreating to his shed
to drink and drink

while we are left to clean up
the mess.

Collecting

    Mum has an Ikea bookshelf crowded
with cookbooks, recipe magazines and scrapbooks
stuffed with food clippings,
    which is odd given her schedule precludes her
from producing these culinary delectations.
I wonder,
why does she persist with this seemingly incongruous habit?

Does appeal lie
in the discipline
    of sourcing texts of interest,
cutting them
into aesthetic or haphazard orderings
    and placing them neatly
with thin bands of glue,
a press of the hands and a sense of accomplishment.

Perhaps it's therapeutic, this practice,
suggesting freer times ahead,
opportunities to concoct these gastronomic delights,
    the entitlement to do as she likes
once work subsides,
    the kids move out

and she has blessed time to herself.

Sprinkled Field

Recent rain

not fierce
    but adequately gentle
has left its mark

through stipples in supple soil
like stomata on leaves

the freshly sowed seed
will sprout,
patches of dirt soon to be swathed

by a uniform sward –
a sea of green.

Ode to Onyx

Two dogs long
    and half a dog high,
he growls unashamedly at man, woman, child
or beast,
no matter how much larger or more imposing.

Fiercely loyal to me,
       his family and home –
he is far too proud to heed command or
instruction.
Any attempt to master a dachshund is futile.

He reclines on me often,
nosing his balayaged body of caramel and coal
into the ruffles of my clothes,
    his ears, long and silken, drape over me,
and when not slumbering, he follows me wherever I venture
around the house,
or
indulges his proclivity for pilfering socks.

His presence placates my anxiety,
    retunes my fitful heartbeat and returns me
to equilibrium. Worries and apprehensions
diminish when holding the silly sausage.

The joy he brings us is
irreplaceable,
beloved canine and counterpart.

Mindfulness

I am not present at this dinner party.
I'm beyond the safety of the room,
    my consciousness disturbed,
somewhere far away
from the canapés and champagne
    and idle conversation with friends
(if they can be called that
when we only meet and converse
once every six months).

Consumed
by an obdurate worry whose kernel has made its home
inside me,
    germinating into a healthy specimen which shoots
sinew and tendon,
to wind through
    and around muscle and organ.

This evening
of retreat, of coming together
has been soured by the taste of my mentor's razor edged
censure
towards my work (deemed to be so shockingly aberrant),
the exertion of living week to week,
of finishing off assignments,
keeping pace with my writing,
        and the existential quandary of always asking what if?

I must breathe,
>   call myself back into the room,
back to its élan,
its aromas and textures. Let this disquiet fall out of my
reptilian core.
As my breath resolves
I suddenly remember the proverb:
not my circus, not my monkey.

Stitches

A tumble from the playground makes
a slit

in the terrain of her young skin,
a deep slice into tissue,
    no wider than an inch (although it's difficult to tell
with so much scarlet spillage).

Snuffling, the needle lances,
her pain subtracted.
    Mum tells her to look away as
the parted skin is sutured

the shiny line to become a route
on the map of her life.

Love Fool

I rush into love. I do. I dive into the newness and splendour of it all, with little regard for the consequences. Impetuous and unashamed. And I expect that I will continue to – in fact, I know I will – leap before I look. I don't consider love attainable by logic – a sum insisting correctness – or achievable through aloof investigation. I think that it demands seizure: brash actions and immediacy. From all the times it's slipped away, I've learned that one can't afford to be cool and calculating. Because even if I plunge after I've jumped, I have implicit faith in the knowledge that, eventually, I will reach a ledge.

Rain on Tin

There it goes,
that inimitable sound:
    tapping
        tapping
like anxious fingers.

I lie in bed,
warm and reposed
enmeshed within blankets,
    exorcised of worry and doubt,
because in this moment
I am contented
falling asleep,
    listening to,
and in the company of
this elemental lullaby.

Forest

A day trip to the mountain of emerald,
cedar and amber pines,
tall and pencil-straight. Having never been,
you surveyed intently the flashing
wonders as we drove.

Walking amongst the florae –
       on needle-encumbered floor –
deep in the belly of the timbers,
we have skirted the prying eyes of others
and talk about everything and nothing,
holding hands
and exchanging kisses
without care or hesitation.

This boy in the forest with me,
    sitting on the moss-mottled trunk,
        I am sure he loves me. A sapling,
new and green,
whose roots could bore deep   and grow.

The sun bleeds through the leaf canopy,
muted rays falling on our faces. It was here,
   only with him,
that for the first time,
I got to feel the sun.

Bubble About to Burst

Orbicular skin
    glistening and multi-hued
existing in midcourse,
hovering
    shuddery,
engenderer of enchantment
descending,
expiry imminent

gone.

Sitting in a Waiting Room

She positions herself well
in the corner chair so no lunatics are contiguous.
    A precarious tower of magazines on the coffee table
is clearly diseased,
the asylum masquerading as a day spa, with its
scented candles and dimly lit ambiance.

She knows
this woman she's seeing
       (not even a doctor)
will start the session by being worldly and
charming and
so very self-effacing.
    She'll ask her if she wants tea or coffee,
and then how she takes it. Her office will be provisioned
with emblematic paraphernalia:
couch,
       credentials (if any),
    bookshelves stacked with obligatory texts,
and a goldfish to foster peace or good feng shui.

A comment
about this unseasonable heat will ensue,
an icebreaker before   this woman
tries to bore into her cagey lobe
       with some Freudian nonsense,
and cast about
for her past's influence on her present actions.

This quack will ask bog-standard questions,
scribble notes on some edgy, urban designed notebook
and say,
'We'll come back to that later.'

In the waiting room, she looks at the others,
all of them thinking they can be fixed
    with potions and tricks
but she knows,
none of them can ever
be free.

Path

My journey has become encumbered from what was a course
of untroubled steps
    light paces on a path that has been a shallow trough
in the earth,
running smooth and chalky from the waterless flow

Mesh of birds' voices around me
        unseen, but somewhere, in the profuseness of the golden trees.
I've come to a crossroad patched with lichen,
    limey and flaky. Forking like a serpent's tongue,
        both courses undulate and disappear into the
hazy void   the luminescent vagueness.
I wasn't anticipating this divergence of route,
the demand of executing choice   so now
    my heart heavies with apprehension.

What adventures and prospects will I avert if I turn
the wrong way (if such a thing exists)?
Can I live
always wondering what may have come from that neglected track,
    be satisfied with a single story,
eclipsed in the overshadow.

Out

The phrase is so tedious and silly –
the idea that people need declare themselves
seems so old hat and ruinous.

Built it into a rite,
a moment
upon which the rest of our lives will hinge;
    one instance of admission,
though I wonder what exactly
we are admitting to, and why
        are we the only ones who must proclaim?

Such disclosure seems like the airing of dirty laundry,
owning up to a indictable action.

We wait to see
if we will still be loved
have a home   after the words
    pass our lips.

Siblings

On this winter day in the park
a little brother and sister are playing
    pirate ships or perhaps it is tiggy.

She trails him,
implicitly,
    kicking up the tanbark and clashing
her invisible sabres against his
in a climatic duel.
They scale the playground, now transformed
    into a battle arena in the infinity
    of their imaginations.

The unshakable allegiance she has
to her brother,
her occasional glances toward him for approval
reminds me how much I venerate
my own sisters,
the sacredness of our trinity,
the unassailable connection
of being our darling mother's children.

Cyclone

Despite the news report two days before,
they were unprepared
when she hit
    (like she cared).

Wind tearing through leaves like the violent combing
of hair;
a haze of shrapnel,   the churn of uprooted fence palings,
roofing
and signs
swallowed them, engulfed them;
the rootedness, the bearings of this town,
scattered like ashes.

The sea surged
and detonated green-grey,
crashing
onto the limestone
    (where moronic youths assembled
for nature's show),
spitting like a cobra, foam and spray.

Time became an illogical notion,
    measurements suspended in the void   as the cataclysm
unfolded
around them –
and afterwards
the prospect of picking up,
       moving the procession of their lives to some peaceful
pasture,
caused more destruction than the caprice
of the grey mistress ever could.

Illusory Highway

Shedding

I am suffocating (have been
for such a long time) under this band's constriction,
    coiling like serpent of silver
from which there is no   deviating.
Tenderness fades like spring's bloom
and obligation is the only bind keeping me here.
But this new one –
       this swain –
summer to the abiding winter I have had
to brave –
the bringer of light   love   laughter,
       the one with whom I have the best chance
       to know happiness.

I imagine telling this one:
eyes glazed with threads
    of fluid crystal,
shimmering white
against the pallor;
the chemical composition
of sorrow.

I am inexpert in breaking hearts.

Question

Asking what one does as a vocation
is no longer acceptable
with so many extraneous whys
and wherefores.

He recalls vividly
the thick sludge of anxiety and shame
working its way around his body
               like toxin –
when someone inquired,
what he does with himself,
    how his days are occupied.

Answering that he currently doesn't do anything,
he is met with a mystified glare –
    a certain look in their eyes.
(Is it repugnance, pity?)
Some hurriedly find a new topic, while others
more unmannerly or
               misapprehending
pursue with some ham-handed segue,
perhaps asking if he's looking for something,
    even menial,

as if the pride and desire of societal engagement
were apparently undesired by him.
    No consideration is given for what it is
that holds him   back.

Piano

The arrival of the piano was an event –
not for me, but for the musically adroit
in the household. Everything was moved
to make way for the ebony contrivance,
which would
stand out against our humdrum décor,
    with its ostentation and loveliness.

Positioned there, tremendously important –
almost threatening –
against the meagre wall,
        light slicing along its crisp edges,
obsidian glass, Narcissus's reflection brought to being
in its lustrous patina.

I am scared to touch
for harm will surely come to it,
but I am startled to see
the Irmler's black and white fingers
embracing
of mine.

Obedient and willing,
it doesn't care about my inexpert
        ordering of notes and rhythm;
    soon we converse like friends,
gratifying one another with the intimacy we share.

On My Skin

When the raindrops touch
my skin
    landing on my upturned palm like a critter –
there is a second when sanities
and perceptions miscarry
and I can't interpret
whether their quick stings of sharpness are
cold   like spines of ice or
sizzling,
like bacon fat
    spitting
out of the pan.

Intellect tells me their must be bitter,
    like melancholic clouds   withdrawn sun,
even so
I am cautious to confirm
when I can't trust what I touch.

Pearl

A bottom dweller startles,
its frantic escape causing a lifting
        of sand from the seabed,
    twirling and
spiralling in a dispersing   cloud
like an ejaculation of pollen into the sugary spring air.

Slowly
the suspension settles, but one wayward grain
departed from its comrades,
      floats   along on intrepid currents
and comes to rest within the mucus lining
of an oyster shell.

The temerity of this irritant –
    unwelcome and unwanted –
causes the oyster to secretes liquescence to coat
           the irksome itchiness of the foreign body.

With repeating linings, the infinitesimal grain begins
to thicken,
      harden
until a lustrous circlet emerges
and comes to rest
on the pillowed body of the oyster –
        a pearl,
treasure of the deep
    precious and rare,
so divorced from its bothersome beginning.

Mind's Making

I always hold onto ideas,
however obtuse or impractical,
    hoping, quixotically, that a meagre germ will sprout
and I will be rewarded with the lush flourishing
(when I write or make art)
of a fully fledged concept
enriched with all the sumptuous details and delicate balance of
evasiveness and tangibility.

I wish the process of creating were scripted –
        like a recipe –
where I need only follow an outlined
              and unfailing method
to yield satisfactory results,
or
        that it were as simple and quick
as letting loose a cage's latch
to allow my thoughts the unfortified freedom of birds.

Instead I've found that forming an idea and then artfully
presenting it
is much like a palaeontological venture,
    intricately carving around the specimen,
(sacred and full of potential)
to release it from its sedimentary confines.

The filtering and sieving of ideas is simply the substrate
for creating.
Like a rampant pests, ideas need be culled.
Still,
I find myself wondering   what might have become
of any idea I chose to abort?

Stay

Night has escaped us,
its hours, fallen, like sand between fingers.
Glancing at the galaxy of
phosphorescent stars on the roof
I asked him if he'll stay.   Splayed out
on my bed – his T-shirt raised,
briefs peeking out   from beneath slipping
skinny jeans –
he says he's never made a home   in another man's bed.
And I tell him I haven't it in me
to let him know.

Onwards

Every time I see him,
Mr Winters is sitting in his wheelchair
by the window of his white-walled
prison,
waiting idly for morning to circle into afternoon,
then slip into night.

He's uninterested in going
to the community room to join the other
frail and breaking bodies,
the useless and indignant.
      He hates it here, he tells me. He needs his sentence terminated.

Embarrassment occurs daily for him:
unable to transport food from hand
to mouth
    or enjoy privacy when he bathes.
His body, a bony frame stretched
within a thin film of skin,
endures such daily tests
without progress.
He's not going to improve.

Instead he must wait
for what the politicians call   'nature'
to dictate when it's time,
           as though such a decision could be theirs to make.
  This is where humanity comes to die.

Letter

Your letter

in ink that runs silky like weeping ebony,
    in the pores of brown paper

is an arrangement of words
brought forth from the

imperceptible dimension of thought
and laid down

in the intransience of time. It is
your voice made corporeal

for my eyes,
when I cannot trust

what my ears have heard.

The Beginning of Desire

Pulled from sleep,
your mind has become displeased with the stasis
of slumber

it must instead occupy these hitherto restful hours
with thoughts of him:
projections
    and wonderings
fantasies
    and possibilities.

Neurons fire like arrows,
    flaming and purposeful,
an entire retuning of the system ensues –

a homeostatic imbalance,
        need and want now indistinguishable,
self   no longer paramount –
cognition is dissolved.

Obsession,
hope,
pain –

a prisoner in your own being.

M

Happily you float
while I drown in the ocean between
us.

Terrifying uncharted waters,
immeasurable in distance   and interspersed
    with a medley of dangers and possibilities.

What lies beneath the teasing white glint
of the berg,
far below its body in the black
and blind sea?

I have been pierced as Saint Teresa had,
enraptured. Wanting
so desperately your lips,
    your eyes,
        your hands.

You are light
parcelled in flesh,
        the thought of your touch, incandescent.
And now everything –
    dreams   hope   life –
hinges upon whether or not your love
will disambiguate the abstract

For nothing is truer than the truth that,
when I'm with you,
I am both blessed
    and stricken.

On My Father

My father disowned me when he found out.
The embarrassment of having a gay son,
        beyond any degree of acceptance
or understanding.

How could he face the blokes at work
    (and what if they found out?).
It must have been easier for him to renounce me,
pass off my existence as an inconvenience –
remove me –
the septic tissue.

Perhaps he thinks I'm less of a man,
    or that I've failed in my masculinity,
that my fornications are licentious,
the quintessence of all stereotypes,
destined for disease and an early grave.

I don't know why he discounts me,
    and my heart isn't compelled to discover.
I've learned to stop
exhausting myself by trying so hard to puzzle it out.
His understanding (should it ever eventuate)
        will not be of my making.

Lesson

Children have that ability –
    sometimes enviable
    sometimes unfavourable –
to be unperturbed in self-expression. They care not
for wandering eyes and what others might think,
having little measure of self-censorship.

Acting maniacal,
voices raised, tantrums brewing,
belching, fighting amongst themselves –
they have no sense of propriety,
       completely uninhibited in their displays
until
    something happens
on the way to maturity
that causes them to close
         like a fly trap
and become more perceptive,
more inclined towards discretion,
reserve,
and hold in what they once had no qualms about
allowing out.

Ministering

A car has pulled over to a charity bin
          (a beacon in the shabby and squalid alleyway)
and a mother and son begin
feeding items
          – toys and bags of clothes –
inside the steel belly.

The eagerness, the joy
of this exchange,
an altruistic transference,
        granting goodness from their self-abnegation.

Silent heroes,
leaving as quickly as they came;
their task complete.

Kiss

Leaning into me,

confident, rushing contact,
lips touching
    firmly,
plunging into the ecology
        of one another.

Joined by our incandescent caress,
sharp   like knives,
    tender as petals,
vane of lip

    you and I
kiss.

Innocence

I sometimes close my eyes and relinquish
this world,
soaring like a bird on some sublime airstream
to another plain
where the child in me likes to play.

How I miss the world
      as seen through the eyes of a child,
the satisfaction in unknowingness,
    when the world still upheld its promise of possibility,
and believing
    was so much easier
than the dark truth
of my reality.

Longing

There is no alternative but to crash
into each other,
intrude through our scared spaces
and infiltrate the borders we've marked
    and guarded
so unwaveringly.

How expert we are in forgoing.

How content we've become
in watching life's projector flash by. Surly you, like I
tire of excelling in such
unfulfilling speciality.

You must know,
that of all the paths I have neglected to tread,
none will have more of an impact,
    will leave a mark more ineffaceable,
than the one I fail to walk
with you.

Ladybird

tiny dot of scarlet
spotted with black

on the green
blade of leaf

no mere bug
though seldom seen

you are adored,
charming, benign flyer

i have no agenda
or wish to ask of you

only that you stay
a little longer

before you
fly away

Habitual

His head rests on the jaundiced pillow,
nearing sleep
    but not quite succumbing,
for nothing entices him into slumber.

Tomorrow the day reiterates,
    as rewind and play are pushed on the machine of his life,
and he wakes bleary-eyed to ready himself for work.

Tomorrow's clothes wait in the bathroom:
starched shirt   crisp and firm,
    pressed pants and polished boots.
No time for breakfast –
maybe an instant coffee if each prescribed minute
is met.

Morning commute
traffic jam, fiery brake lights,
then the same conversations with colleagues –
        water cooler monotony.
He returns home: 6.14 p.m.,
assemble, haphazardly, the components of the evening's meal

Clearing messes   suds, washcloth and tea towel,
    returning utensils to their compartments,
flicking through the TV channels,
retiring to the bedroom.

His head rests on the jaundiced pillow,
nearing sleep
    but not quite succumbing,
for nothing entices him into slumber.

Dollhouse

I'm watching my niece play with her dollhouse.
    More than a triangular box to her,
it is a logical arrangement of compartmentalised spaces,
each with its own assigned function and decoration: curtains,
furniture, amenities.
With arbitrary but decisive ordering,
                she assigns certain dolls to certain rooms,
    unaware of gender roles or the inharmonious interaction
between the colour palette of poppets and their space.

I wonder how long it will be
before she comes to know that the world is not as
regimented,
nor systematised
as this flimsy construction would have her believe.

Will her heart, now open and receptive,
become just a little tarnished
when she learns some of us will always be dolls:
the playthings of others,
    manipulated by their will,
and with our freedom limited.

For now, it's best to let her play.

Cornell's Boxes

Bits from the world

picked and placed
in paint-blotted punnets

meaningless, frugal fragments
fusing together

to form a narrative –
the voice of some unnamed soul.

A history,
a life,

alluded within
a shadowbox treasury:

each piece seemingly simple,
perplexedly random.

Yet I see such care in the ordering,
the precision of the items;

the genius of Cornell.

Next To Him

he drifts to sleep beside me
for the first time

and I, too nervous to slumber,
lie and listen

to the rise and fall
of his breath. His nocturnal body

draped by the white sheet
turns, and my breathing,

my heartbeat,
attempt to syncopate with his

as I curl
like an ancient ammonite

against the arched rim
of his youthful form.

Incoming

Wind flurries on the avenue,
leaf and litter coasting

stems sashaying,
then,

the thick droplets fall,
pedestrians retreat:

rain on broiled concrete
releases that metallic smell.

Her Grandmother's Necklace

Her grandmother had a rose gold necklace,
ornate in design,
a bequest that been filled
with the lives of its owners for over a century.

I remember the braid of metal
        gliding between her arthritic
fingers,
watching the chain move fluid and snakelike
down the jowly skin of her neck,
        stippled with freckles,
above the faint,
midline incision

The stone (jade or
aquamarine)
        in the centre of the
charm,
was perfectly circular,
    refracting the light to produce
a dazzling play of colour
        that would make even the most brilliant
rainbows bow their arc
in deference.

Fast Boy

you've changed quite a lot
during these few years

standing there
        now a man
trimmed in the finery of a tailored suit

the party circling around,
you in the corner,
knocking back the love fool hopefuls

no need to part the maddening crowd
reintroduce myself;
i'm called away

you were always too bold,
too bright
to notice me.

Dramaturgic

Quiet spectacle is his forte.
His subdued charisma
      unconsciously
   calls attention not through ostentation
(he reviles notice)   but by his
poise
   and allure.

There is no brazen theatricality here,
no bellicose performance of body   or voice.
He is instead
a quiet storm,
   contained,
      the most dangerous kind
      perhaps.

Gran's Chair

I never knew my great-grandmother.
All I have to offer me some connection to her
and my antecedents,
is a fireside chair
    (Art Deco I believe)
        with olive green tone and geometric form

It bears the attrition of this bygone era,
nevertheless, it is effective
    in enwrapping the sitter in its velour skin,
offering the comfort
personified by this woman,
by all accounts gentle
        gracious.

Your Face

When I truly see your face, not merely glance upon it, I'm reminded that I look at exquisiteness besting any sculptor's skill. Your cheeks are frames of chalky white cliffs, running long and wide into a shoreline of smooth skin. Centred, your nose is slim and linear: proffering direction on how to navigate the haunting beauty of the ethereal landscape. But when I meet your eyes, as blue and untameable as the sea, I am swept out. There is no protest or fighting back against the carrying. I am taken to a destination unknown. Here, in the nameless vastness, thoughts are abandoned. There is no time. No passing. There is only you. And here, I'll swim gladly.

Tea

Capsule of parched leaf in papery membrane
bungee jumping from a fraying thread
between fingertips

impatient whistle of the kettle –

Plunging,
staining the volume of this boiling soak;
fingers glide up
       and down
directing this marionette parcel.

Dark with intense flavour;
plop of sugar, two in fact,
splash of milk;
    a whirlwind mid-cup, lightening to perfect creamy colour

the afternoon ritual.

Moonlit Room

Moonlight spills
lunar liquid in the house,
      seeping through niche and chink,
to graduate the sleek, secret black,
which retreats   back
to the still and heavy waters of shadow.

Weaving its incantatory
spell,
it sinks,
    into the abyss.
        Lines dance in the light,
mesmerising
white blue
    blue white.

Flower

The flowers in the garden droop their heads
heavy and contrite

fan of petals crinkle
into pleats of pinkness

brilliance wanes
and closes

under the first crackle
of winter frost.

Moh

A ravenous mouth
satisfying unknown hunger.

    You screamed colour,
the man with coffee eyes
and skin
brushed with the ochre of far away princes. I know
you
don't know what you want,
are waiting for the picture to sharpen,
    break
from the mist   clear   clean
crisp.

I am cut by those jagged pieces
of indecision
and bleed.
No stitches, no tourniquet can stopper
the outpouring. Soon I will be spent.
My crumb of hope won't sustain,
won't appease this hunger.

You both made me
and broke me.

Later

They said to use you
as poultice,
write you in my poems

as though you weren't already there

catalytic,

rousing
every line,
in every stanza.

I am the pen
and you drive the words

you always have.

www.ingramcontent.com/pod-product-compliance
Lightning Source LLC
Chambersburg PA
CBHW070914080526
44589CB00013B/1290